Goodword

Islamic

A Graded Course
Grade 8

Mohammad Khalid Perwez

GOODWORD

Goodword Books Pvt. Ltd.
P. O. Box 3244, Nizamuddin P. O., New Delhi - 110 013
E-mail: info@goodwordbooks.com
First published 2006
Reprinted 2007   Printed in India
© Goodword Books 2007

goodwordbooks.com

CONTENTS

Chapter 1 — The Quran: The Base of Islam

The Quran is the Holy Book which was revealed by Allah to the Prophet Muhammad ﷺ. It is the most beautiful gift to mankind from its Creator. It is known by many names, among which are *Al-Furqan* (the criterion), *Al-Huda* (guidance), *Al-Mufassal* (the fully explained), etc. and its meaning is 'reading'. The Quran contains the Divine Words of Allah who is the Creator and the Sustainer of the universe and all that it holds. These words were revealed through the Angel Jibril (Gabriel) to the Prophet Muhammad ﷺ. It is a manual for mankind to lead a contented and honest life. It has instructions from God to human beings, showing them the clear path of chastity, honesty and faithfulness. The mission of the Quran is to direct creation from darkness to light—to the Way of the Almighty and Most High Allah.

Why does Allah want us to follow this chosen path? It is because He loves us more than anybody else does, even more than our parents, brothers and sisters or teachers do! Allah wants us to be happy and successful in this life and in the life after this one, so He gave us the means to find that happiness and success by believing in Him and what He has revealed in the Holy Qur'an.

The Quran is a treasure-trove of knowledge presented to us by that Majestic Sovereign Lord, Allah. It is like a bouquet of divine flowers whose sweet smell, if we breathe it in deeply, purifies our souls. When we speak with this knowledge, we speak in the language of peace, goodness and respect, because we start living by those ideals which Allah has fixed for us.

The Quran is the Book of Ultimate Wisdom and Truth. It provides inspiration for those who seek justice and knowledge in life. Allah has shown us the steps to achieve enlightenment and salvation through accepting what we have been given and rejecting what we have been forbidden. We must aspire to live up to the expectation of our Lord and He helps us by giving us clear guidance in the Quran.

The Quran also contains stories of past prophets like the Prophet Adam علیه السلام, the Prophet Nuh or Noah علیه السلام, the Prophet Ibrahim or Abraham علیه السلام, the Prophet Sulayman علیه السلام, Solomon علیه السلام, the Prophet Dawud or David علیه السلام, the Prophet Isa or Jesus علیه السلام and others. Through their stories, we are taught and admonished not to go astray, as that would earn the anger and punishment of Allah.

Allah is our Creator and Master; therefore, He cares for us and has sent His messengers (prophets) to warn and give glad tidings of

His Mercy and Might. These honourable men were given the task of providing the tools necessary to save creation from despair and faithlessness by encouraging us to learn about loving, worshipping and obeying the One True God.

The Quran is the guiding spirit that takes us to the heights of righteousness. By following the Qur'an, we live with strong values and with the noble purpose of serving Allah. We can thus become moral and responsible human beings who embody the attributes of love, honesty and faith. Allah says in the Quran, 'This Book is not to be doubted. It is guide for the righteous, who have faith in the unseen and are steadfast in prayer; who bestow in charity a part of what We have given them; who trust what has been revealed to you and to

others before you, and firmly believe in the life to come. These are rightly guided by their Lord; these shall surely triumph.' (Surah 2:1)

The fundamentals of Islam are based on the teachings of the Quran. The Quran is the Divine Book of Laws, the principles of which are laid down in the most explicit terms in the Quran itself. The essence of the teachings of the Quran is the faith in Islam as it was professed by the Prophet Muhammad ﷺ and taught by him to all mankind.

An Eternal Concept

This universe is the creation of Allah. He has made this universe and everything in it with some purpose. Allah created the earth, the sky, the sun, the moon, the stars and many more things which are all under His command. All bow to Allah in complete submission and strictly follow the routine laid down for them by Him.

As Allah says in the Quran:

> *"To Allah bows all that is in the heavens and on earth, whether living creatures or the angels, for none are arrogants before their Lord." (16:49).*

Allah created the first man and the first prophet, Adam, and from him came the Children of Adam ﷺ (*Bani Adam*) which denotes mankind. Allah gave the human soul the ability and natural disposition to accept Allah as his Master and to follow His dictates. This was Islam—an eternal religion which demanded recognition of Allah as the one God whose command was obeyed by everything in this universe. Whenever human beings forgot this teaching, Allah sent prophets to remind them of this eternal concept.

EXERCISES

1. Fill in the blanks

a.   The meaning of the word Quran is _____. (Laws/Reading)

b.   The Quran is the Book of Ultimate _____. (Wisdom/Language)

c.   Allah has sent his _____.(Messenger/Messengers)

d.   The Fundamentals of Islam are based on the teachings of the _____.
     (Quran/ Hadith)

e.   This _____ is the creation of Allah.(World / Universe)

f.   Islam is an _____ religion. (eternal/ old)

2. Match the Columns

Column A	Column B
Al-Huda	The fully explained
The Quran	Guidance
Al-Furqan	Reading
Al-Mufassal	The criterion

3. Answer the following questions

a.   Who revealed the Quran and what does the Quran contain?

b.   Give any three names of the Quran. What do they signify?

c.   What do you understand by Islam?

4.   Divide the class in the groups of four and discuss – why the Quran is the most beautiful gift to mankind. The discussion can be in the light of the daily life. Every group has to make a report. A student from each group can read out the report in the class.

5.   Identify and recite at least three Surahs which describe the importance of the Quran in our lives. Make a note of them.

Chapter 2   Oneness of Allah (*Tawheed*)

Islam is built on five pillars. They are called the *arkan* of Islam, which are the five basic duties which all Muslims must perform. They are not the whole of Islam but without them Islam would not

really exist. These five *arkans* are like the 'pillars' which support the edifice of Islam. If any of the 'pillars' is weak, the whole building (Islam) suffers.

These five pillars are *Shahadah, Salah, Saum, Zakah and Hajj.*

Acknowledgement of Allah as one's Lord and Master *(Shahadah)*

Shahadah is the first pillar of Islam, without which the rest is meaningless. The word *Shahada* derives from the word *Ashhadu* which means "I declare" or "I

bear witness". *Shahada* states: *Lailaha Illalahu Muhammadur Rasoolullah* (There is no God but Allah and Muhammad is the messenger of Allah).

Shahadah is acknowledgement of Allah as one's Lord and Master and the Prophet Muhammad as the messenger of Allah. When the individual declares *Shahadah* and truly believes it in his heart, he becomes a Muslim, after which it is around Allah alone that all his thoughts and emotions revolve. He places his complete trust in Allah, therefore, his every action is directed towards earning Allah's favour. When he acknowledges God as his Lord and Master, he enters into a contract with God, a covenant which excludes all other beings and makes Him all in all. To declare *Shahada* is to have faith in one who is Creator, Master and Sustainer of the universe and to accept that the Prophet Muhammad ﷺ is the messenger sent by Allah. Allah sent all His messengers to teach mankind the path that would lead them to salvation. Allah revealed the Holy Book, the Quran to the Prophet Muhammad ﷺ, who was the last of His messengers. When a man fully accepts *Shahadah* he cannot but attribute all greatness to Allah and lead all his life according to the *Sunnah* or the tradition of the Prophet Muhammad ﷺ.

EXERCISES

1. Fill in the blanks

a. If any of the five Pillars of Islam is weak, the whole building (Islam) _____ . (suffers/ does not suffer)

b. The first pillar of Islam is _____ . (Salah/ Shahada)

c. The Prophet Muhammad ú was the _____ messenger of Allah.
(one of the / last)

d. When a man fully accepts Shahada and leads all his life according to the _____ (Sunnah/ way of his parents)

e. Shahada states _____.
(I declare / *Lailaha Illallahu Muhammadur Rassolullah*)

2. Match the Columns

Column A	Column B
Arkan	The tradition of the Prophet Muhammad.
Shahadah	God
Messengers	Pillars
The Creator	declaration
Sunnah	The prophets

3. Answer the following questions

a. What are the five pillars of Islam? What do you understand by 'If any of the pillars is weak, the whole building of Islam suffers?

b. Define *Shahadah*.

c. What does *Shahadah* demand of a believer?

4. Divide the class in four groups and have an in depth discussion on *Shahadah* and each group should share their views with the rest of the class. After the discussion everyone should write what they understand from the discussion.

Chapter 3

Prayer *(Salah)*

Salah is a kind of prayer which a Muslim must perform five times in a day. *Salah,* or the five daily prayers, constitutes the second pillar of Islam. During *Salah* everything else in life is set aside for a few moments and Muslims concentrate solely on Allah, praising Him, thanking Him, and asking for His forgiveness and blessing. *Salah* is regarded as a duty that must be performed even if at work, at home, on a journey or even at war.

A Muslim is not supposed to omit his prayers on any account. When a Muslim is too ill to stand or kneel, he can go through the motion of the prayer in his heart while sitting or lying down and reciting the words. A Muslim must begin to practice *Salah* when he is about seven years old, and by the age of twelve it is expected of him as a duty.

When the time for *Salah* comes, Muslims perform a ritual cleansing which is called *wudu* (ablutions) after which they make their way to the mosque, where they all assemble and pray. The prayer is led by an Imam. The *Salah* has various stages; standing, bowing, kneeling and self-prostrating before God. In assuming these various postures, the congregation demonstrate their submission to the Lord.

During the *Salah ayats* or verses from the Quran are recited. Besides this, the prayer includes praise and remembrance of God, supplications to Him and the expression of goodwill towards the Prophet and all believers. *Salah* is said in the Arabic language, the language of the Qur'an.

Salah, as well as being a ritual mode of worship, is an expression of the inner realities of humanity and devotion to God. The ultimate acknowledgment of Allah's greatness is the repetition of the words *Allahu Akbar*, which means '*Allah is the Great*'.

The Call to prayer

You already know that Muslims are supposed to pray five times in a day. These prayers are said at appointed times. At these times, a call to prayer is made by a man who is called a *muezzin*. A *muezzin* can be any person, not necessarily a man specially appointed for this purpose. He must know how to make a call to prayer. The call to prayer is called *adhan* in Arabic. It was instituted by the Prophet after his arrival in Madinah in 623 CE. When the call to prayer is made, everyone hearing it should repeat its words softly.

You must know the words of *adhan*. Here they are given with their meanings in English.

Allahu Akbar – *Four times*
(Allah is Great)

Ashhaduall Ahilaha illallah – *twice*
(I bear witness that there is no god but Allah)

Ashaduanna Muhammadurasullullah – *twice*
(I bear witness that Muhammad ﷺ is the prophet of Allah)

Hayya alas-salah – *twice*
(Come to salah)

Hayyaalalfalah – *twice*
(Come to success)

Allahu Akbar – *twice*
(Allah is Great)

Lailaha illallah – *once*
(There is no god but Allah)

After the completion of *adhan*, everyone must say the following *dua:*

*Allahuma Rabba hadhihiddawatit-tamaati
wassalawaatil quaimati aati Muhammadanil
waseelata wal fazeelata wab'ashu maqamamma
hamoodanil-ladhi wa'adt ahu*

*Allah! Lord of this perfect call and of salat to be offered
presently, vouchsafe Mohammad ﷺ the way of approach
unto Thee and also excellence and elevate him to the
glorious position which Thou hast promised him.*

Prescribed Conditions for Prayer

There are five conditions which have to be fulfilled for salat to be valid.

    a.   Cleanliness or *Taharat*

    b.   Ablutions or *Wudu* (*ghusl*)

    c.   Time

    d.   Dress (covering of *satr*)

    e.   *Qiblah* (direction of worship)

Let us learn about each topic mentioned above.

a.   Cleanliness (*Taharat*)

Taharat can be defined as a state of physical cleanliness. Allah directs us in the Quran to maintain a state of *taharat,* or cleanliness. Muslims have been commanded by Allah to remain clean at all times but more so during *salah,* for *salah* cannot be performed without acquiring *taharat* or cleanliness. In the Quran in *surah 9 at tauba,* verse 108, it is mentioned that Allah loves those who make themselves pure.

The last prophet of Allah has also stressed the need to be particular about personal hygiene. The holy Prophet ﷺ said: "Cleanliness is half the faith" (Bukhari and Muslim).

Therefore, it is necessary for every Muslim to know what criteria Islam has laid down for being clean. There is no question of personal likes and dislikes, one can achieve cleanliness only by the methods taught by Islam for this purpose.

There is some *najasat* or pollution whose presence in one's body makes one impure or unfit to offer *salah*. Its removal by the prescribed method is necessary to be able to revert to the state of *taharat* required to offer *salat*.

b. Ablution (*Wudu*)

After the call to prayer has been made, all Muslims are required to start the preparation for prayer. *Salaha* is an act of worship which is performed in a state of ritual cleanliness. This state is brought about by *wudu* or ablution, which is cleaning oneself with water in a particular manner. By performing *wudu*, one acquires not only physical cleanliness, but also the pure and clean state of mind which is so necessary for performing *salah* with humility. *Wudu* is performed with water, but in circumstances where water is unavailable or its use is detrimental to health, one is allowed to do *tayyamum*, which is done with sand or clay. Allah sees one's intention, not just one's deeds. Islam allows concessions to its followers in any difficult situation. *Tayamum* is one such concession and in difficult situations it is equal to doing *wudu*. It produces the same kind of cleanliness as one achieves after performing *wudu*.

The manner in which *wudu* should be done was explained to the Muslims by the Prophet Muhammad ﷺ. You must already know how to perform *wudu*, however, it would be good to highlight the obligatory actions (*faraed*) in *wudu* for you.

1. Washing of the full face.
2. Washing of both arms from the fingertips up to and including the elbows.
3. *Masah* of at least one quarter of the surface of the head from the forehead.
4. Washing of both feet up to and including the ankle bones.

It would also be good for you to know the *sunnah* in *wudu*. These actions were carried out by the Prophet Muhammad ﷺ while performing *wudu*, therefore, highly recommended for the Muslims.

1. Reciting *bismillah hir Rahman nir Rahim* before starting *wudu*
2. Using *miswak* for cleaning the teeth.
3. Starting with the right hand, arm and foot.
4. Doing everything three times except the *masah* (passing wet hands over the head)
5. Passing the fingers of one hand through the fingers of the other. This is called *khilal*.
6. Washing with due care with the intention of cleaning rather than as a mere formality.
7. Maintaining the given sequence of actions.
8. Using water carefully and not unnecessarily wasting it.
9. Reciting the following *dua* at the completion of *wudu*: *Ashhada an lailaha illallah wahdahu la sharika lahu wa ashhadu anna muhammadan abdahu wa rasulahu.*'

You know that one can perform *salah* after *wudu* as long as one's *wudu* is valid. There are a few actions which invalidate *wudu*. In such a situation one has to stop one's *salah* and again do the *wudu*, then complete one's *salah*.

The following actions invalidate *wudu*:

1. Sleeping with support. However, dozing while sitting without support or during *ruku* or *sajdah* for a moment or two does not render the *wudu* invalid.

2. Unconsciousness for any reason.

3. Touching of the private parts directly.

4. Touching the opposite sex, including kissing.

5. Laughing during *salat*.

6. Passing of wind from the body.

7. Discharge and flow of blood, puss, etc.

8. Profuse vomiting.

c. Time

Salah or the five daily prayers are said at appointed times. Based upon the revelations of the verses of the Quran, the frequency and timings of *salah* were laid down by the Holy Prophet. *Salat* offered within these timing is called *Ada*, i.e. offered in time. If somebody fails to perform *salat* at these timings, he is permitted to offer *Qadha* salat i.e. salat performed at times other than appointed times.

18

However, it is imperative for Muslims to offer *salat* within these timings in congregation in the mosque. Offering *salat* individually is an exception under circumstances beyond the control of an individual. Muslims are supposed to say these five daily prayers in congregation in a mosque and not let these prayers become *Qadha*. However, ladies are permitted to offer *salah* at home individually.

There is a hadith in Sahih al-Bukhari which highlights the importance of saying *salah* at the appointed times. It tells of Abdullah bin Masud asking the Prophet Muhammad ﷺ, "Which deed is the dearest to Allah?" He replied, "To offer prayers at their stated fixed times." He then asked, "What is the next in goodness?" He replied, "To be good and dutiful to your parents." He again asked, "What is the next?" He replied, "To participate in jihad in Allah's cause."

In the Quran also, Muslims have been exhorted to say *salat* at fixed times. Allah says in the Quran in *Surah an-Nisa* in verse 103:

> *"Indeed prayer at fixed hours have been enjoined on the believers." (4:103).*

We understand that you must already know the timings of the five mandatory daily prayers. However, you should also know that there are some specific times when offering *salah* is not approved of. It is considered *makruh* or undesirable to offer *salah* at these forbidden timings. However, under exceptional circumstances, offering *salah* at these undesirable timings is permitted in order to avoid *salah* becoming *Qadah*.

The timings at which *salah* is undesirable are as follows:

1. After offering the *Fajr* Prayers till the sun rises.

2. During the rising of the sun.

3. At noon when the sun is at its zenith

4. After offering *salat al-Asr* until sunset

5. During the setting of the sun.

There is a hadith in *Sahih* al-Bukhari about these forbidden timings. Ibn Umar said, "Allah's messenger said, 'Do not offer *salat* (prayer) at the time of sunrise and at the time of sunset.'"

d. Dress for *Salah*

Salah is an act of worship to Allah, therefore, it is necessary for the worshipper to wear clothes befitting this occasion. They should be free of all filth and pollutants and lend dignity to the appearance of the person. Islam attaches great importance to dress by including it in the prescribed condition of *salat*. It expects people to dress decently and be dignified without being extravagant and showy. It does not approve of obscenity or indecency in public places, the more so during the pious duty of worship by human beings. Such an act would indeed be a degradation of the highest status accorded to them out of all the creations of the universe.

Satr

Allah has prescribed a minimum standard for the covering of the body for worshippers. A worshipper has to cover certain parts of the body failing which his *salat* will not be accepted. Those parts of the body which must be covered properly during *salah* is called *satr*.

Satr for Men

The minimum requirement for men to be able to perform prayer is that they should be covered from the navel to the knee, because for men, their body parts from the navel to the knee constitute their *satr*.

Satr for women

In the case of women, their whole body is considered s*atr*, except the hands (up to the wrists) and face (excluding ears and hair). Therefore, a woman must cover her entire body, except the face and hand up to the wrists during *salah* and at other times also, because Allah says in the Quran in *Surah an-Noor* that believing women should draw their veils over themselves and not display their beauty. Therefore, Islam teaches women to dress modestly and maintain *hijab* in their daily lives. *Salah* being an act of personal worship to Allah, requires the upholding of the correct dress code as taught by the Prophet Muhammad ﷺ.

e. *Qiblah*

The *Qiblah* is the direction in which the Holy Kabah is located. Muslims are supposed to offer their *salah* facing towards the Kabah. This is evident from the Quranic injunctions revealed by Allah in verse 144 of the *Surah al-Baqarah*.

Allah says: "Turn then your face in the direction of the sacred mosque, wherever you are, turn your face in that direction."

The Kabah is the Holy House of Allah. It is the first house on earth built solely for the worship of Allah. It is thus a symbol of monotheism or *tawhid* in Islam and also of the unity of the mission of all the prophets of Allah. It also symbolises the unity of the Muslim community. Muslims, therefore, pray neither to the east nor to the west, but to Allah alone in the direction of the *Qiblah*. By laying down the direction of our five daily prayers, Allah has laid down the real orientation of our lives which is the remembrance and consciousness of Allah.

Every Muslim should strive to say his prayers in the direction of the Kabah. However, on journeys and in dangerous situations, a worshipper may pray in any direction convenient to him. One should not miss or postpone *salat* in a situation when one is not sure of the direction of the Kabah. One must offer prayers in the direction one feels to be the *Qiblah*.

EXERCISES

1. Fill in the blanks

a.   Salah is regarded as a duty that _____ be performed even at war.
     (must/ must not)

b.   Salah is an expression of the _____ realities of humanity and devotion to God. (inner/ outer)

c.   During Wudu, Masah must be done_____Time(s). (three/ one)

d.   The one who gives the call to prayer is called a _____(Qazi/ Muezzin)

e.   Those parts of the body which must be covered during Salah is called _____. (fatr / satr)

f.   In the Qur'an also, Muslims have been exhorted to say salat at _____.
     (five fixed times/anytime).

2. Match the Columns

Column A	Column B
Qadha	Kabah
Allahu Akbar	Bending position in *salah*
Qiblah	Missed prayer peformed at other times.
Satr	God is great
Najasat	Undesirable
Ruku	Minimum covering of the body during *salah*
Makruh	Pollution

3. Answer the following questions

a.   Define *salah*.

b.   What is the call to prayer?

c.   What are the prescribed conditions for a valid *salat*?

d.   Discuss the concept of cleanliness or *taharat* in Islam.

e.   What are the obligatory actions and sunnah in *wudu*?

f.   What is *satr*?

g.   At what times is the performing of *salah* undesirable?

4.   In the light of *Salah* have a class discussion on the importance of prayers with discipline in Islam. After the discussion everyone should write about it.

5.   The students have to recite the Ayaats said in the *Salah*. After that the teacher should explain their meanings and significance.

6.   Every student should maintain a monthly chart for the teacher to check whether they are regularly praying five times a day or not.

Chapter 4

Fasting *(Saum)*

Saum is ritual fasting in the month of Ramadan, the ninth month of the Muslim lunar calendar. *Saum* is the third pillar of Islam. The period of fasting each day lasts from the first light of dawn until sunset. *Saum* is the deliberate control of the body by an act of will. A real conscious effort must be made to make sure that no evil deed is committed or any bad thought is entertained.

If the emotions of the heart or mind, or the behaviour of the Muslim are wrong, then the fast will lose its real significance. This physical abstinence from food and control over behaviour strengthen one's capacity for patience and fortitude. *Saum* teaches us self-control and how to overcome greed and laziness.

God has bestowed innumerable blessings upon man in this world. But man does not see them for the great blessings that they are. It is only when he observes the ritual of fasting that he truly realizes their significance and has a proper sense of gratitude for them. It is in the evening, after a day of hunger, thirst, exhaustion and discomfort, when a man consumes food, that his awareness of God's bounty is most intense. One of the aims of *Saum* is to teach precisely this kind of restraint and patience. The life which a believer is required to live on earth is, from beginning to end, a life of patience. He must confine himself to what is lawful and keep his distance from what has been decreed unlawful by the Almighty. The whole life of a believer is, in a sense, a life of fasting: he is required to abstain not just from food and drink but from anything which is wrong. He is also to refrain from attempting to make lawful anything which God has disallowed.

Do's and Don'ts in *Saum*

We should first know what the aims of *Saum* are. *Saum* is without doubt a great act of deliberate control of the body at the command of God. Accordingly, it is worthy of an immense reward from Allah. The significance of Ramadhan has become known to us through the sayings of the Prophet Muhammad ﷺ. There is a hadith according to which Allah says: "The fasting person has left off his food, drink and desires for My sake. The fast is for Me. So I will reward him for it and the reward for good deeds is multiplied ten times."

The aims of *saum* are to:

* develop self control;
* develop sympathy for the poor;
* refrain from passion; and
* gain spiritual strength.

While observing *saum*, one has to follow some do's and don'ts. It should be the aim of every believer to observe *saum* as best as he can. Since it is compulsory for the adult Muslim to observe the fasts of Ramadhan, it would be useful to know at this point how one should observe these fasts, so that they are accepted by Allah.

Here are some do's while observing *saum*.

Do's

* Saying all prayers in congregation in the mosque.

* Saying all *nawafil* prayers.

* Reciting from the Quran as much as we can.

* Doing *dhikr* of Allah all the time.

* Reciting *darud* frequently when not saying *salat* or reading the Quran.

* Giving in charity and feeding the poor.

- Inviting the poor and needy on *iftar* and dinner.

- Inviting one's relatives and friends on *iftar*.

- Saying *tarawih* prayers at night after *isha*.

- Saying *tahajjud* prayers, especially on all *lailatul Qadr*.

- Giving *fitr* before the end of the Ramadhan.

Here are some don'ts which one must observe if one wants one's fast to be valid and accepted by Allah.

Don'ts

- Telling lies

- Foolish behaviour

- Fighting

- Abusing

- All evil actions

- Sexual acts

There are conditions in which Muslims are meant to omit fasts. But these fasts omitted under difficult conditions are supposed to be made up later. Those who are old and weak are, however, excused from fasting, and they should, in order to earn Allah's reward provide food for the needy, if they can afford it.

The people mentioned below can omit their fasts:

- The old and the weak
- Pregnant and nursing mothers
- Children below twelve years
- Those who are sick
- Those who are on a journey

Voluntary Fasting *(Nawafil Saum)*

There are some *saum* which, though not being *fard*, i.e., compulsory, were kept by the Prophet Muhammad ﷺ. Hence these are highly recommended for Muslims.

These fasts are:

- The fast of Ashura
- The fast of Yaume-Arafa

EXERCISES

1. Fill in the blanks

a. Fasting is observed from dawn till _____. (noon / dusk)

b. Fasting enables us to _____ spiritual strength. (gain / lose)

c. We should give fitrah _____ the end of ramadhan. (before / after)

d. Allah says: "The fast is for my sake. So I will reward him for it and the reward is _____. (multiplied ten times / ten times).

e. There _____ in which Muslims are meant to omit fasts.
   (are conditions / are not any conditions)

f. An adult who misses fasts, must make up by keeping _____. (one / all fasts)

2. Match the Columns

Column A	Column B
Saum	Powerful nights
Dhikr	A special prayer during Ramadhan
Tarawih	Breaking of fast
Tahajjud	Voluntary fasts
Lailatul Qadr	Remembrance of Allah
Iftar	Fast
Nawafil saum	A special prayer said before dawn

3. Answer the following questions

a. What is the importance of *Saum* in Islam?

b. Discuss the do's and don'ts in Saum.

c. What is *nawafil saum*?

4.. Every student should write their individual experience of realizing any of the aims of the Saum, during fasting.

5. There should be a class discussion on how observance of Saum helps us to understand Islam and brings us closer to Allah.

Chapter 5

Almsgiving *(Zakat)*

Zakat (alms-giving) is the fourth pillar of Islam. *Zakat* is given out of one's savings and wealth at a minimum fixed rate of 2.5% per annum. This is a religious duty performed by every Muslim who has savings at the end of the year. The word *'Zakat'* means to purify or cleanse. The aim of paying *Zakat* is to keep one's wealth from becoming a source of greed and selfishness. It is also a test of Muslim honesty when it comes to expenditure. *Zakat*

is meant to cleanse the heart of the love of money and the desire to cling to it. Money is for the service of humanity and for promoting good and justice in the world.

Zakat gives a clear indication of what one's responsibilities to others should be. Everyone is expected to sympathize with those afflicted by adversity. *Zakat* brings the realization that all of one's possessions are gifts from God and makes one more keenly aware of the virtues of devotion to God. *Zakat* is a reminder that a selfish stance is a wrong stance, and that others must be given their rightful share from our earnings. God chooses whom to make rich or poor. The wealthy are obliged to give to the poor. Only by giving something away for the sake of God will one appreciate its true value. Society should be so ordered that those fortunately placed in life should come to the assistance of the less fortunate. Such a society, in short, is a haven of contentment and well-being.

Nisab

Nisab is defined as the minimum amount of capital or wealth such as gold, silver, minerals, treasures, crops, fruits, cattle and articles of merchandise, below which *zakat* is not applicable. In order to come within the purview of *zakat,* one must possess property or capital in excess of this minimum exemption limit for a whole year.

The *nisab* is normally expressed in terms of quantities of two metals, i.e., gold and silver and not in terms of the value in any currency. For the sake of convenience, the prescribed quantities of the specified quality of gold or silver are to be worked out at prevailing prices to determine the minimum amount which attracts the provision of *zakat.* However, *nisab* for agricultural produce and domestic cattle (not for sale) is different. The ownership of wealth for a period of less than a lunar year does not attract the provisions of *zakat.* This condition is not applicable in the case of agricultural produce, where it is due immediately after each harvest.

Zakat is considered as a form of worship, which is expressed through the distribution of material wealth. *Zakat* is mandatory on all those Muslims who have surplus wealth exceeding a specified limit. The offering of *zakat* pleases Allah immensely. It leads to self-purification of

those who pay *zakat;* they receive manifold rewards from Allah both in this world and in the Hereafter. There are serious warnings to the defaulters in payment of *zakat* both in the Holy Quran and the sayings of the prophet.

The assets on which *zakat* is due

The Prophet Muhammad ﷺ laid down the following items upon which *zakat* is applicable.

- Gold and silver
- Cash
- Stock in trade, *i.e.* items for sale
- Agricultural produce
- Domestic cattle (specified)
- Minerals and treasures

There are some items of household use on which there is no *zakat,* unless they are made of gold or silver. These are:

a) Kitchenware, cutlery, crockery, furniture, fixtures, fittings, sanitaryware, etc.

b) All types of vehicles for own use or for commercial use

c) Houses/flats for own use or for the purpose of letting out

d) Land and plots not for sale.

Rate of Zakat

The rate of *zakat* is common for all assets valued in cash, except agricultural produce, cattle and minerals. It is 2.5% (one fortieth part) of the total cash-value of prescribed assets.

When the value of the qualifying assets is equal to or more than the prescribed *nisab*, *zakat* is assessed taking the whole value into account.

Gold: Standard 24 carat is taken into account for the purpose of *zakat*. The *nisab* in the case of gold is laid down at 87.300 gram. The equivalent quantity of 22 carat gold works out to 95.236 gm.

Silver: For the purpose of *zakat*, silver of 99% purity is taken as standard. The *nisab* of silver is fixed at 611.100 gram.

Cash: Cash held in banks, financial institutions and contributory funds attract *zakat*.

The following should be considered as cash.

a) Currency of any denomination and country provided it is legal tender.

b) Cash in banks or financial institutions

c) Equity shares, debentures, investment certificates, negotiable instruments like promisary notes, bills of exchange, banker's cheques, mutual funds or any such instruments as can be converted into cash.

Agricultural Produce

Zakat is applicable to all kinds of grains and fruits which can be stored and preserved like wheat, paddy, pulses, dates, figs, etc. Agricultural produce obtained from free irrigation by natural means like rains, rivers, lakes, etc., are taxed at the rate of 10% of the total marketable produce. On account of this rate, *zakat* on agricultural produce is commonly referred to as *ushr*, meaning a tenth in Arabic. In the ease of agricultural produce obtained by artificial means of irrigation for which the farmers has to incur expenditure for digging wells, installation of pumps and payments of irrigation cess, etc. the rate of *zakat* is fixed at 5% of the total produce.

The Spirit of Zakat

Zakat is the fourth 'pillar' of Islam. *Zakat* means setting apart for God every year a certain portion of one's savings and wealth (generally 2.5 percent) and spending it upon religious duties and on needy members of the community. The fulfilment of this duty is, in fact, a kind of reminder that all one has is in trust from God. Man should, therefore, hold nothing back from God. To whatever one may amass in one's lifetime, one's own personal contribution is insignificant. If the Supreme Being, who is at work in the heavens and on the earth, refused to co-operate with man, there would be nothing that the latter could accomplish single-handedly. He would not be able to plant so much as a single seed to make things grow. Nor could he set up any industry, or carry out any other such enterprise. If God were to withdraw from us His material blessings, all our plans would go awry, and all our efforts would be brought to naught.

Zakat is the practical recognition of this fact through the expenditure of money for the cause of God. Islam requires man to consider his personal wealth as belonging to God and, therefore, to set apart a portion for Him. No maximum limit has been prescribed, but a minimum limit has definitely been fixed. According to statutory *zakat*, each individual must abide by this and spend a fixed minimum percentage of his wealth every year in the way prescribed by God. While spending from his wealth, he is permitted neither to belittle the recipient nor to make him feel obliged or grateful to himself. His wealth must be given to the needy in the spirit of it being a trust from God, which he is making over to the genuine titleholders. He should feed others so that he himself is fed in the Hereafter, and he should give to others so that he himself is not denied succour by God in the next world.

Zakat is a symbol of one's duty to recognize the rights of others and have sympathy with them in pain or sorrow. These sentiments should become so deep-rooted that one should begin to regard one's own wealth as belonging, in part, to others. Moreover, one should render service to others without expecting either recognition or recompense. Each individual should protect the honour of others without hope of any gain in return. He should be the well-wisher of not just friends and relations, but of all members of society. *Zakat*, first and foremost, makes it plain to people that their entire 'possessions' are gifts of God, and, secondly, dissuades the servants of God from living in society as unfeeling and selfish creatures. Indeed, throughout their entire lives, they must set aside some portion for others.

We must serve our fellow human beings only in the hope of receiving a reward from God. We must give to others with the divine assurance that we will be repaid in full in the next world. In a society where there is no exploitation, feelings of mutual hatred and unconcern cannot flourish. A climate of mutual distrust and disorder is simply not allowed to come into being; each person lives in peace with another, and society becomes a model of harmony and prosperity.

On the legal plane, *zakat* is an annual tax, or duty; in essence and spirit, it is recognition on the part of man of the share which God, and other men, have in his wealth.

(The article, "The Spirit of Zakat" is gleaned from the book, *Islam As It Is* by Maulana Wahiduddin Khan)

EXERCISES

1. Fill in the blanks

a. The word *zakat* means to _____. (clarify / purify)

b. We pay *zakat* _____. (yearly / two-yearly)

c. The rate of *zakat* is _____ of the total cash value of the prescribed assets. (2.5% / 5.5%).

d. The minimum capital on which *zakat* becomes due is called _____.
    (nisab / hisab)

e. *Zakat* is mandatory on all those Muslims who have _____.
    (surplus wealth / wealth)

f. Giving something away for the sake of _____ will one appreciate its rue value. (Allah / Society)

2. True or False

a. *Zakat* is not obligatory on Muslims.

b. *Nisab* is expressed in terms of the quantity of gold or silver.

c. *Zakat* purifies our wealth.

d. There is no *zakat* on minerals and treasures.

e. Agricultural produce obtained by natural means of irrigation attracts a *zakat* of 10%.

3. Answer the following questions

a. Discuss *zakat* and how it purifies our assets.

b. Define *nisab*.

c. List the items on which *zakat* is due.

d. What do you understand by the 'rate of *zakat*'?

4. There should be a class discussion on Zakat and how it can tackle the problem of poverty in the society. After the discussion every student should write what they understand from it.

Chapter 6

Hajj

Hajj is the fifth pillar of Islam. It is the pilgrimage to Makkah made between the 8th and 13th of *dhulhijjah*, the twelvth month of the Muslim lunar calendar. If a Muslim goes on the pilgrimage to Makkah at any other time, it is known as *Umrah*, or the lesser pilgrimage, and the significance is not the

same as *hajj*. *Hajj* is compulsory for all adult Muslims who have the wherewithal and good health to undertake the journey.

The most important moment celebrated in *hajj* is the occasion when the loyalty of the Prophet Ibrahim عليه السلام was put to the test by Allah. The Prophet Ibrahim عليه السلام passed the test and Allah called him Ibrahim *Khalilullah,* the friend of Allah.

The *hajj* rituals include circumambulations or *tawaf* around the Kabah, the wearing of *ihram*, walking seven times between the hills of Safa and Marwa, the casting of pebbles at the

stone devils, standing at the mount of Mercy or Jabal ar Rahmah. There are many other rituals which are the sunnah or tradition of the Prophet Muhammad ﷺ.

The experience of hajj performed in the midst of hundreds of thousands of people gives one a unique spiritual feeling. When the words of *the talbiyah* are recited by the pilgrims clad in *ihram*, a unique humbling experience is felt by them, which leaves many of them shedding tears of joy on being physically present there, ready to answer the call of Allah.

Labbaik Allahumma Labbaik
Labbaik Lashirka Laka Labbaik
Innal Hamda wanni matalaka wal mulka
La Sharika Laka.

The English translations of the words of the *talbiyah* are:

"I respond to Your call and
I am obedient to Your orders.
O Allah, Here I am!
O Allah, I respond to Your call and
I am obedient to Your orders.
You have no partner, I respond to Your call.
All sovereignty is Yours.
And You have no partners with you."

The Elements of *Hajj*

Hajj has four basic constituents:

1. assuming the state of *ihram*, i.e., wrapping oneself up in two sheets of unstitched cloth,

2. presenting oneself on the plains of 'Arafah,

3. *tawaf al-ifadah* (circumambulation of the Kabah on the Day of Sacrifice),

4. *as-sa'y* (walking at a brisk pace or running between the mountains of Safa and Marwah in Makkah).

Ihram with due intention:

The pilgrim puts aside his normal clothes and wraps himself up in two unstitched sheets and thus assumes the garb of piety. (*Ihram* for women, however, consists of their covering the entire body except the face.) Having thus wrapped himself up in two sheets of cloth, the pilgrim affirms his intention thus:

I affirm my intention to undertake the pilgrimage and deny myself all the things forbidden during these observances, for the sake of Allah.

He then offers two rak'ahs *of salat and addresses Allah thus:*
Here I am, O Allah, to do my pilgrimage.

The *ihram* has to be put on before the pilgrim crosses the *miqat* (a point fixed at a certain distance on each of the roads leading to Makkah).

Ihram, which is just two sheets of unstitched white cloth, one wrapped around the waist, and the other over the left shoulder, symbolizes equality, single mindedness and self-sacrifice. The idea of all men living on earth as God's servants, and therefore as equals, is expressed in the wearing of ihram. In this way all artificial, discriminatory barriers are broken down between people from all walks of life.

Wuquf (standing or halting) at 'Arafah:

The pilgrim has to halt on the plains of 'Arafah all or part of the day and night beginning on the 9th of *Dhu'l-Hijjah,* after the sun begins to decline, before noon, until dawn on the 10th of the month. The pilgrim, during this period, has to engage himself in reciting the formula affirming his readiness to respond to Allah's call for *hajj* and expressing his humility before Allah in terms appropriate to the solemn occasion.

Tawaf al-Ifadah

This is an obligatory ritual in which the pilgrim makes seven circuits of the Kabah after returning from the plains of 'Arafah, and remembers Allah (may He be glorified) in appropriate terms.

As-Sa'y between Safa and Marwah:

This ritual entails the pilgrim going at a fast pace to cover the distance between Safa and Marwah seven times. While doing so, he remembers a similar coming and going undertaken by the mother of the young Isma'il عليه السلام in quest of food and drink for her baby.

In case any one of the basic rituals mentioned above is neglected or left out, the pilgrimage will be deemed not to have taken place.

Halting at Muzdalifah

Muzdalifah lies between Mina and 'Arafah. Pilgrims offer the shortened combined prayers of *maghrib* and *'isha* after the afternoon crimson on the horizon has vanished. They do it on the eve of the Feast of Sacrifice. They also perform their *fajr* (early-morning) prayer at this holy place, then set out for Mina before sunrise, in due humility and remembrance of Allah.

Stoning the Pillars (*ramyu al-jimar*)

Throwing pebbles at the Pillars is the symbolic disavowal of the Evil One from the bottom of one's heart at a place where Satan had appeared to the Prophet Ibrahim عليه السلام in order to deflect him from his determination to sacrifice his son Isma'il عليه السلام in obedience to the command of Allah. The pilgrim begins by throwing seven pebbles at *jamrat al-'aqabah*.

Shaving the hair or shortening it

The pilgrim has to either completely shave off or shorten the hair on his head, after having thrown the pebbles at the largest of the three stone pillars on the Day of Sacrifice. This accomplished, the pilgrim comes out of the state of *ihram* and all things lawful in ordinary life become permissible for him except the sexual act.

'Umrah (the Lesser Pilgrimage)

Performing *'umrah* is one of the important precepts of the Prophet ﷺ. It comprises four observances namely, (i) *ihram*, (ii) circumambulation (circling round the House), (iii) running (*sa'y*) between Safa and Marwah (iv) shaving/shortening the hair.

It must be pointed out here that each ritual connected with the pilgrimage needs a detailed discussion, as there are certain prophetic traditions and practices as well as formulas for supplication to Allah and remembrance of Him which can be studied in specialized books on religious observances in Islam.

Things forbidden during *ihram*

It is not allowed for a person in a state of *ihram*, be it for *hajj* or *'umrah,* to put on stitched clothes or use cosmetics or other means of adornment for the body or indulge in hunting or go to women until he has shaved off his hair or shortened it. There are a number of other commandments for both men and women in this regard, some of which are given below:

A man, for example, is not allowed to cover any part of his head or put on any clothes other than the two unstitched sheets, one for the upper part and the other for the lower part of the body. He is also not allowed to use perfume or trim his nails or cut any part of his hair. The sexual act is also forbidden for him.

A woman, on the other hand, will be deemed to have entered the state of *ihram* only if she covers her entire body (and head) except the face. Her *ihram,* thus, comprises the uncovering of her face. She is also forbidden to use any cosmetics, etc. as long as she is in a state of *ihram.*

A person turns an unbeliever under Islamic law if he (i) denies the obligatory nature of *hajj* (ii) ridicules the rituals and observances connected with *hajj* (iii) either inveighs against the House of Allah or tries to degrade it in people's esteem or seeks to defile and desecrate it with the intention of belittling its importance.

EXERCISES

1. Fill in the blanks

a. Hajj is performed between _____(8ᵗʰ to 13ᵗʰ / 9ᵗʰ to 13ᵗʰ Dhulhijjah).

b. Hajj is compulsory for all _____(adult / aged muslims).

c. The prophet Ibrahim passed the test and Allah called him _____(khalilullah / kalimullah).

d. Innal Hamda wanni matalaka _____(wal mulka/ labbaik).

e. The pilgrim has to halt on the plains of the day and night beginning on the _____(9ᵗʰ / 10ᵗʰ of Dhu'l-Hijjah).

2. True or False

a. *Sa'y* is walking briskly between Safah and *Mawah*.

b. Ihram consists of four sheets of unstitched white cloth.

c. The *talbiyah* is recited during *salah*.

d. Standing on the plains of Arafat is called *wuquf*.

e. Muzdalifah lies midway between Mina and Arafah.

3. Match the Columns

Column A	Column B
Tawaf al-ifadah	The son of the Prophet Ibrahim ﷺ
Safa and Marwah	The 12th month of the Muslim lunar calendar
Dhulhijjah	The circumambulation of the Kabah on returning from Arafah.
Jamarat al-aqabah	The hills near the Kabah.
The Propeht Ismail ﷺ	The Stoning pillars.

4. Answer the following questions

a. What is *hajj*?

b. Write down the words of the *talbiyah*.

c. What are the constituents of *hajj*?

d. What are the things forbidden during *hajj*?

e. What is *umrah*?

5. The class should be divided into four groups and discuss the significance of Hajj and how every act of it's highlights the basic teachings of Islam. Every group should write its views and read it out in the class.

Chapter 7   A Compiler of Hadith

Imam Malik

Imam Malik Ibn Anas, whose ancestors originally came from Yemen, was born in Madinah in the year 715 CE. Imam Malik is regarded as one of those great scholars of *hadith* whose interpretation of the Quran and the *Sunnah* form the basis of the laws known as *fiq,* or school of thought, in Islam. Apart from the *fiq* of Imam Malik, there are three other *fiqs* in Islam which are known as Hanbali *fiq,* Shaafi *fiq* and Hanafi *fiq.* Imam Malik was a *taebeen* — he had met

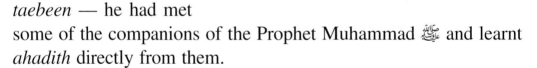

some of the companions of the Prophet Muhammad ﷺ and learnt *ahadith* directly from them.

Imam Malik received his education in Madinah, which was then the most important seat of learning. Imam Malik was highly attracted to the study of law and devoted his entire life to the study of *fiqh*. He acquired his knowledge of the Prophet's sayings from the *Sahaba*.

Among Imam Malik's writings is the great work entitled *Kitab al-Muwatta,* which is the earliest surviving book of Islamic law and hadith. It contains the sayings as well as the practices of the Holy Prophet ﷺ as observed by his Companions in Madinah.

Al-Muwatta, which means 'the approved', is acknow-ledged as the most important among Imam Malik's writings. It is reported that Malik showed his book to seventy jurists of Madinah and every single one of them approved of it, so he named it *al-Muwatta* (the approved). About *al-Muwatta*, Shah Wali Allah said that it was the principal authority of all four schools of law.

Imam Malik held the *hadith* of the Prophet Muhammad ﷺ in such reverence that he never narrated anything nor gave a *fatwa* without first performing his ablutions. Imam Malik was famous for his piety and integrity and he courageously stood up for his convictions and was prepared to suffer for them. Imam Malik was publicly flogged by the governor of Madinah for refusing to take the oath of allegiance to the Caliph al-Mansour on a matter which was based on a false *hadith*. However, when al-Mansour learnt of this outrage, he apologized to the Imam and dismissed the governor.

Later when Caliph Haroun al-Rasheed visited Madinah at the time of *hajj*, he summoned Imam Malik to visit and deliver a lecture. Imam Malik refused to go to the ruler and instead invited him to attend the class in which he delivered regular lectures. The Caliph accepted the invitation and, accompanied by his two sons, sat among the students to hear the Imam's lecture.

Imam Malik died in the year 795 C.E. at Madinah and was buried in the cemetery of al Baqie in Madinah.

Some Ahadith from al-Muwatta

Malik related to me from Zayd ibn Aslam that the Messenger of Allah, may Allah bless him and grant him peace, said, "Give to a beggar even if he comes on a horse."

Yahya related to me from Malik from Nafi from Abdullah ibn Umar that the Messenger of Allah, may Allah bless him and grant him peace, said from the mimbar when mentioning sadaqa and refraining from asking, "The upper hand is better than the lower hand. The upper hand is the one which expends, and the lower one is the one which asks."

Malik related to me from al-Walid ibn Abdullah ibn Sayyad that al-Muttalib ibn Abdullah ibn Hantab al-Makhzumi informed him that a man asked the Messenger of Allah, may Allah bless him and grant him peace, "What is backbiting?" The Messenger of Allah, may Allah bless him and grant him peace, said, "It is to mention about a man what he does not want to hear." He said, "Messenger of Allah! Even if it is true?" The Messenger of Allah, may Allah bless him and grant him peace, said, "If you utter something false, then it is slander."

Yahya related to me from Malik from Ibn Shihab from Ali ibn Husayn ibn Ali ibn Abi Talib that the Messenger of Allah, may Allah bless him and grant him peace, said, "Part of the excellence of a man's Islam is that he leaves what does not concern him."

Yahya related to me from Malik that he had heard that the Messenger of Allah, may Allah bless him and grant him peace, said, "I was sent to perfect good character."

Yahya related to me from Malik from Salama ibn Safwan ibn Salama az-Zuraqi that Zayd ibn Talha ibn Rukana, who attributed it to the Prophet, may Allah bless him and grant him peace, said, "The Messenger of Allah, May Allah bless him and grant him peace, said, 'Every deen has an innate character. The character of Islam is modesty.'"

Yahya related to me from Malik from Ibn Shihab from Ata ibn Yazid al-Laythi from Abu Ayyub al-Ansari that the Messenger of Allah, may Allah bless him and grant him peace, said, "It is not halal for a Muslim to shun his brother for more than three nights, that is they meet, and this one turns away and that one turns away. The better of the two is the one who says the greeting first."

EXERCISES

1. Fill in the blanks

a. Imam Malik delivered his regular lectures at _____. (Makkah / Madinah)

b. About Al-Muwatta, _____ said that it was principal authority of all four schools of law. (Shah Wali Allah / Imam malik)

c. The Prophet Muhammad said, "Give to a beggar even if he comes _____." (of full hands / on a horse)

d. The Prophet Muhammad said, " Part of the excellence of a man's Islam is that he leaves what _____." (does not concern him / is not in Islam)

e. The Prophet Muhammad said, "Every deen has an innate character. The character of islam is _____." (honesty / modesty)

2. True or False

a. The book of hadith which Imam Malik compiled was known as *Al-Muwattah*.

b. Imam Malik's ancestors came from Iraq.

c. Imam Malik is buried in Makkah.

d. *Tabaeen* were those who had met the companions of the Prophet Muhammad and learnt ahadith directly from them.

3. Match the Columns

Column A	Column B
The birth of Imam Malik	A school of thought
Haroun al-Rasheed	715 CE
Al-Muwatta	An Abbasid Caliph
Fiq	Ahadith book compiled by Imam Malik

4. Answer the following questions

a. When and where was Imam Malik born?

b. Name the four schools of thought or *fiqs* in Islam.

c. Which famous caliph attended along with his sons the lecture of Imam Malik in Madinah?

5. Divide the class in seven groups and ask them to discuss one hadith each which are mentioned in the chapter. After the discussion a student from each group should read out the report written by their group.

6. The teacher should give a theme to each student like love, discipline, friendship and ask students to collect three hadiths each and next day they should share it with the class.

Chapter 8 | The Story of the Prophet Isa علیه السلام

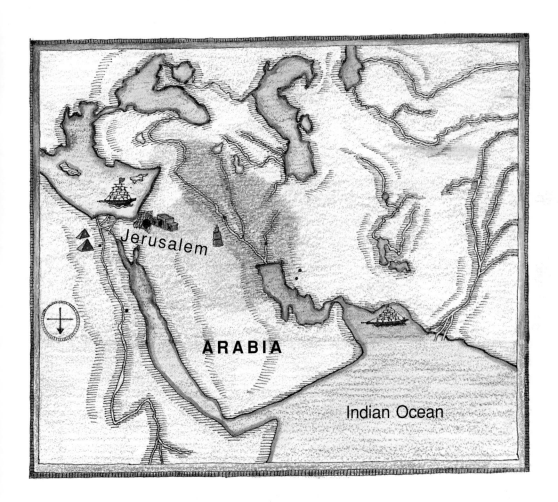

The Prophet Isa علیه السلام or Jesus

The Prophet Isa علیه السلام, a prophet of Allah, was born without a father by a miracle of Allah. He was the son of Maryam, or Mary, a pious devoted lady described as a virtuous woman in the Quran. The birth of the Prophet Isa علیه السلام was a miracle and a sign of Allah's power. However, it was no more miraculous than the creation of the

Prophet Adam عليه السلام and Eve, who had neither father nor mother. Allah creates whatever He wants; if He wills something, He has only to say, "Be," and it is.

The Quran tells us about Maryam, the mother of the Prophet Isa عليه السلام. She is honoured in the Quran and referred to as a chaste woman,

a servant of Allah, chosen by Allah, purified and raised as a righteous and pious women. The Quran mentions that when Maryam was born, her mother dedicated her to the service of Allah. Allah graciously accepted her and made her grow in purity and beauty and gave her into the care of the prophet Zakariya عليه السلام, who was an old man and childless at that time. Later, the Prophet Zakariya عليه السلام prayed to Allah to grant him a child and Allah accepted his prayer and Yahya عليه السلام was born to him, despite his wife being barren.

Maryam was a humble and devoted servant of Allah. This is stressed in the Quran when Maryam is ordered to worship Allah, to pray to Him, and prostrate herself before Him.

The Quran says: "Behold! The angels said: O Mary! God has chosen you and purified you—and exalted you above the women of all nations. O Mary! Worship your Lord devoutly: Prostrate yourself, and bow down (in prayer) with those who bow down." (*Surah al-Imran*, 3:42)

When Maryam grew up, Allah sent an angel to her who said: "Nay, I am only a messenger from your Lord, to announce to you the gift of a holy son." Maryam said in disbelief: "How shall I have a son, seeing that no man has touched me, and I am not unchaste?" The

Angel replied, "So it will be, says your Lord, 'that is easy for Me. And We wish to appoint him as a sign unto men and a mercy from Us."

And so Maryam conceived and then retired to a remote place to suffer the pangs of childbirth and deliver her child all alone. Allah performed a miracle and provided her with a rivulet near her, and a palm tree with fresh ripe dates on it.

When Maryam brought her child to her people, they were amazed and said, 'O sister of Aaron, your father was not an evil man, nor was your mother unchaste.' Helplessly, Maryam pointed to her child, the infant Isa عليه السلام, who said, "I am indeed a servant of God: He has given me Revelation and made me a prophet. And He has made me blessed wheresoever I may be, and has enjoined on me prayer and charity as long as I live. He hath made me kind to my mother and not overbearing or miserable. So peace is on me the day I was born, the day that I die and the day that I shall be raised up to life (again)." (Surah Maryam 19:27-30).

This was a sheer miracle – an infant speaking to the people— but this was the promise Allah made to Maryam when He sent the Angel Jibril to announce to her the birth of Prophet Isa ﷺ. According to the Quran, the Angel Jibril (Gabriel) said: "He shall speak to the people in childhood and in maturity and he shall be (of the company) of the righteous."

Allah taught the Prophet Isa ﷺ the Book and Wisdom and the Law and the Gospel. The Prophet Isa ﷺ preached his people to have true faith in Allah, the One and Only, and in His messengers and in His Holy Books, which He revealed to His prophets.

Allah told the Prophet Isa ﷺ to announce to his people: "I have come to you with a sign from your Lord, in that I make for you out of clay, as it were, the figure of a bird and breathe into it, and it becomes a bird by God's leave: and I heal those born blind, and the lepers and I quicken the dead by God's leave, and I declare to you what you eat and what you store in your houses. Surely therein is a sign for you if did believe."

The Prophet Isa ﷺ confirmed the previous Holy books of Allah revealed to the prophets Ibrahim ﷺ, Musa ﷺ and Dawud ﷺ. He taught people: "It is Allah who is my Lord and your Lord; then worship Him. This is a way that is straight."

The Prophet Isa ﷺ, the son of Maryam, was a prophet of Allah, and this was the message which the Prophet Isa ﷺ taught his people to believe in. But the people differed among themselves and believed that the Prophet Isa ﷺ was the son of Allah. The Quran is replete with commands from Allah mentioning that Allah is the One and Only: it does not befit the Majesty of Allah that He should beget a son. When Allah has to create anything, He only says: 'Be' and it is. Allah says in the Quran:

> *"Jesus is like Adam in the sight of God. He created him of dust, then He said unto him. 'Be,' and he was." (Surah 3: verse 59).*

The Quran says that the Prophet Isa ﷺ, the son of Maryam was only a messenger of Allah. He was no more than an apostle. Many were the apostles that passed away before him. Allah says: "He (The Prophet Isa ﷺ) is nothing but a slave on whom we bestowed favour, and we made him an example for the children of Israel." (Surah 43:59).

Allah made Maryam (or Mary) and her son, the Prophet Isa ﷺ, a sign for all people.

Allah sent the Prophet Isa ﷺ with clear signs of His sovereignty. The Quran says: "When Isa came with clear signs, he said: Now have I come to you with wisdom, and in order to make clear to you some of the points on which you dispute: therefore fear God and obey me."

Allah denies in the Quran that the Prophet Isa ﷺ was crucified. In fact Allah raised the Prophet Isa ﷺ to Himself. The Quran says:

> *"They declared: 'We killed Christ Jesus, the son of Mary, the apostle of God'—But they neither killed, nor crucified him. But so it was made to appear to them.... Indeed no, God raised him up to Himself, and God is Exalted in Power and Wise." (Surah an-Nisa, 4:157-58).*

Allah also says in the Quran that the Prophet Isa ﷺ will be sent back to the earth on the Last Day just before the Resurrection, when he will destroy the false doctrine, that spread in his name and prepare the way for the universal acceptance of Islam.

The Quran says, "And (Isa) shall be a sign (for the coming of) the Hour (of judgement): therefore have no doubt about the Hour, but follow you Me: this is a straight way." (Surah Az-Zukhruf 43:61)

The Prophet Isa عليه السلام all his life preached Islam to people, told them to follow the scriptures which were sent before him and the Book which had been revealed to him by God. The Prophet Isa عليه السلام also prophesied the coming of the Prophet Muhammad صلى الله عليه وسلم, the last Prophet of Allah. The Quran says: "And remember, Isa, the son of Maryam, said: O Children of Israel, I am the apostle of God (sent) to you confirming the law (which came) before me, and giving glad tidings of an apostle to come after me, whose name shall be Ahmad." (Surah As-saff, 61:6)

EXERCISES

1. Fill in the blanks

a. Maryam was given in care of the prophet _____. (Zakariya ﷺ/ Yahya ﷺ)

b. Prophet Isa ﷺ said, "I am indeed a _____ of God. (servant / messenger)

c. Prophet Isa ﷺ said with God's leave I declare to you what you eat and what you _____. (have in your hearts / store in your houses.)

d. Prophet Isa ﷺ gave glad tidings of an apostle to come after me whose name shall be _____. (Muhammad / Ahmad)

2. True or False

a. The Prophet Isa ﷺ was born without a father.

b. Maryam was the aunt of the Prophet Isa ﷺ.

c. The Prophet Isa ﷺ prophesied the coming of the Prophet Muhammad ﷺ.

d. Allah did not raise the Prophet Isa ﷺ to Himself.

3. Match the Columns

Column A	Column B
The Prophet Zakariya ﷺ	The book of Allah revealed to the Prophet Isa ﷺ.
The Bible	An angel of Allah who brought revelation to the prophets.
Jibril	A prophet of Allah asigned to take care of the Maryam (or Mary).
The Prophet Adam ﷺ	The Prophet who will be raised up to life again.
The Prophet Isa ﷺ	The first prophet of Allah born without a father and a mother.

4. Answer the following questions

a. Explain how the Prophet Isa's ﷺ life was full of miracles and a sign of Allah's power.

b. Who was Maryam? What did her mother do when Maryam was born?

c. Who was the Prophet Zakariya ﷺ and what did he pray to Allah?

d. What was the message which the Prophet Isa ﷺ spread? Discuss how it continues in the teachings of Islam.

Chapter 9

The Conquest of Makkah

When the treaty of Hudaybiyyah was signed in the 6th year of
the *Arabic hijra* between the Prophet Muhammad ﷺ and the Quraysh,
certain tribes came under the protection of the Muslims, while the
others sided with the Quraysh. It was decided that no tribes would
attack each other or fight with one another. Exactly one year after
the treaty, the Prophet ﷺ and his Companions came to Makkah to
perform *umrah*. As per the treaty, the Quraysh vacated the city and
the Muslims performed the *umrah* peacefully. One of the results of
the treaty of Hudaybiyyah was that the relations between the Quraysh
and the Muslims became peaceful, which gave the Muslims a much-
needed respite and the freedom to reach out to more and more people
to present Islam to them. The Quraysh and others also reflected on
the happenings since the proclamation of Islam by the Prophet ﷺ.
The more they thought, the more they became convinced about the
authenticity of the call of the Prophet ﷺ. When the Muslims were

performing *umrah*, the Quraysh watched them from the hilltop and were awestruck at the simplicity and dignity of their way of performing *umrah*. Besides this, the teachings of Islam to shun all vices and immoral behaviour, and its emphasis on honesty, and righteous behaviour did have an impact on the Quraysh. As a result, a few of the prominent Makkans like Khalid ibn al-Walid, Amr ibn al-As and the guardian of the Kabah, Uthman ibn Talhah, embraced Islam, followed by a large number of people from Makkah. The Muslims grew stronger day by day, whereas fear and weakness crept into the ranks of the Quraysh.

In the 8th year of the *Arabic Hijra*, in clear violation of the Hudaybiyyah treaty, the Quraysh incited their ally, the tribe of the Banu Bakr, to attack the Muslims' ally, the tribe of Khuzaah. In a surprise attack on the tribe of Khuzaah by the Banu Bakr with arms supplied by the Quraysh, a number of men from the Khuzaah tribe were killed. When the news of this flagrant breach of the treaty reached the Prophet ﷺ, he sent word to the Quraysh that either they should pay compensation for the murders or that they should withdraw

their support from the Banu Bakr. If not, they should withdraw from the treaty. The Quraysh replied that they held the treaty null and void. On hearing this, the Prophet ﷺ decided to conquer Makkah. He sent word to the Muslims all over the peninsula to mobilize at once.

Meanwhile, the Muslim army proceeded to Makkah under the command of the Prophet Muhammad ﷺ, whose aim was to conquer the city without any bloodshed. This army had more men than Madinah had ever seen before. So many Muslim tribes had joined in such great numbers and with such armaments that the wide expanse of the desert was filled with them. They moved fast, and at every stop, many more tribes joined their ranks and added to their armaments and equipment. Every soul was filled with the faith of Islam and entertained no doubt that Allah's help would bring them victory.

The Muslims reached al-Zahran, four miles from Makkah, where the Prophet ﷺ decided to camp for some time. Meanwhile Abbas Ibn Abdul-Muttalib, an uncle of the Prophet ﷺ and a non-Muslim living in Makkah, took all the members of his family, and went out in the direction of Madinah and met the Prophet at al-Juhfah and converted to Islam. Al Abbas saw that the Muslim armies were so great in number that the Quraysh would be no match for them. He became apprehensive of the fate of the Quraysh people and asked the Prophet ﷺ what the Prophet ﷺ would do in case the Quraysh asked for a guarantee of its own security. The Prophet, keen on preventing any bloodshed, urged him to tell the Makkans that they should reconcile themselves to the Muslims before they took Makkah by storm.

Al Abbas rode on the Prophet's ﷺ white mule and went towards Makkah. He met Abu Sufiyan on the way and brought him to the Muslim camp. Since Abu Sufiyan was on the prophet's ﷺ mule, nobody did him any harm. Faced with the threat of death, Abu Sufiyan converted to Islam. The Prophet ﷺ announced that whoever laid down his arms, sought refuge in Abu Sufiyan's house, or stayed indoors, or entered the Mosque would be secure.

The Muslims thus entered and occupied Makkah without any opposition; only the front assigned to Khalid Ibn al-Walid put up any resistance. This area was populated by the most hostile and antagonistic members of the Quraysh. Many of them were the attackers of Khuzaah tribe. When Khalid's army entered their quarter, they showered it with arrows. Khalid, however, quickly dispersed them losing two of his men, but killing thirteen of them.

The Prophet ﷺ praised Allah and thanked Him for the conquest of Makkah. He then camped on a height opposite the mountain of Hind. The Prophet ﷺ was moved by the sight of Makkah, he rode towards the Kabah on his she-camel, al Qaswa, and circumbulated the Kabah without dismounting. He then called upon Uthman Ibn Talhah to open the Kabah for him. All idols kept in the Kabah were destroyed. The Holy Prophet prayed inside the Kabah. Thereafter, he thus addressed the people of Makkah:

"There is no deity but God. He has no associate. He has fulfilled His promise, He has helped His servant and has, by Himself, broken up all groups, Yes, all vanity, all revenge, old demands for blood-revenge, all blood moneys—these are all now trampled under my feet. The only exceptions are the continued trusteeship of Harame-Kabah and the provision of water for the Hajis. O Quraysh! Allah has destroyed (for good) the vain notions, and the pride of heritage of the days of *jaahilya*. All are children of Adam and Adam was created from dust."

After that the prophet recited from the Quran:

> *"O Men! We have created you from male and female and constituted you into peoples and tribes that you might know and cooperate with one another. In the eye of God, the highest among you is the most virtuous. God is omniscient and all powerful."*

He then asked the Quraysh: "O men of the Quraysh, what do you think I am about to do with you?"

"All that is good," they answered, "for you are a noble brother and a noble nephew of ours."

The Prophet ﷺ then said: "Rise, then, and go. For you are free."

EXERCISES

1. Fill in the blanks

a.   The treaty of Hudaibiyyah was signed in the _____.
     (4th year of the *Arabic hijra* / 6th year of the *Arabic hijra*)

b.   The Muslims camped at _____ during their march to Makkah.
     (Zahran / Abwa)

c.   The Quraysh sent _____ to Madinah to talk to the Prophet ﷺ.
     (Abu Sufian / Ikrimah)

d.   Abbas ibn Abdul Muttalib converted to Islam _____ the conquest of
     Makkah. (before/after)

e.   Allah has destroyed(for good) the vain nations, and the pride of heritage
     of the days of _____. (jaahliya / quraish)

f.   In the eye of God, the highest among you is the _____. (most
     high in rank / most virtuous).

2. True or False

a.   After the treaty of Hudaybiyyah, the Khuzaah tribe came under the
     protection of the Makkans.

b.   The Banu Bakr tribe killed the men of the tribe of Khuzaah.

c.   The Prophet ﷺ wanted to conquer the city of Makkah without any
     bloodshed.

d.   Khalid Ibn Walid was the commander of one section of the Muslim army
     which entered the city at the conquest of Makkah.

e.   The Prophet ﷺ announced a general amnesty to the people of Makkah
     after the conquest of the city.

3. Answer the following questions

a.   Write briefly about the treaty of Hudaybiyyah.

b.   Write briefly about the result of the treaty of Hudaybiyyah.

c.   Who violated the treaty of Hudaybiyyah?

d.   Describe briefly the conquest of Makkah by the Prophet ﷺ.

4.   A class discussion should take place on the address of the Prophet
     Muhammad ﷺ to the people of Makkah. Highlight how it summarizes
     Islamic teachings and defines the path in future to be taken by Muslims.

Chapter 10

Islamic Society

The Rights of the Orphan

The Quran says: "Do not oppress the orphan." (Surah 93:9). Allah has commanded all Muslims to treat the orphan with love and affection. Orphans need our special care and attention. We need to give them our best help and support so that they may not end up being exploited. There is a saying of the last prophet of Allah, Muhammad ﷺ: 'Even passing a hand over the head of an orphan with love and affection is an act of charity.'

The Quran is full of injunctions on the fair treatment of the orphan. On innumerable occasions the Quran has exhorted Muslims to take great care of the orphans in society, and especially if an orphan is one of their own relatives. Then it becomes the moral and religious duty of every member of the family in question to take care of him.

The Quran says in surah 9: verses 14-15: "Those whom Allah loves, give food on a day of privation to the orphan with claims of relationship."

The Quran relates those who deny the Day of Judgement with those who reject orphans.

"Have you observed him who denies the Day of Judgement. That is one who repels the orphans." (Surah 107: verses 1-2)

It can be inferred from the above verses that Allah abhors those who repel orphans as much as He abhors those who deny the Day of Judgement—one of the fundamentals of a Muslim's faith. Denying the Day of Judgement amounts to unbelief and Allah has likened the oppressor of the orphan to an unbeliever.

Exploitation of the orphan can lead to serious evils in the society. Allah in many places in the Quran has given the general commandment to believers to follow His commandments with regard to the orphan.

Allah says in surah 4: verse 36: 'Show kindness to parents, and to near kindred, and orphans, and the needy.'

'Spend your wealth, out of love for Him, on your kin, on orphans, and on the needy' (Surah 2: 177)

The rights of an orphan are considered sacrosanct in Islam. Those who do not honour the rights of the orphan will bring down upon themselves the wrath of Allah both in this world and in the Hereafter. Allah says in the Quran: "Those who devour the wealth of orphans wrongfully, do but swallow fire into their bellies." (Surah 4:10)

At another place in the Quran, it says, "Restore the property of the orphans to them (when they reach maturity) and do not substitute your worthless things for their good ones and do not devour their wealth by mixing it up with your own. For this indeed a great sin."

The Quran mentions that among the virtues of a righteous person is his love of feeding the poor, the indigent and the orphan for the love of Allah.

Haram and *Halal*

With the advent of Islam, certain legal principles were established which determined what was lawful (*halal*) and what was prohibited (*haram*) in a Muslim's life. The principle established by Islam is that the things which Allah has created and the benefits derived from them are essentially for man's use, and hence are permissible. Nothing is *haram,* or prohibited, except that which is prohibited on the basis of a sound and explicit verse of the Quran or a clear, authentic saying of the Prophet Muhammad ﷺ.

This principle is derived from freedom of action, according to which nothing may be restricted except what Allah has restricted. This is because commanding and prohibiting are both in the hands of Allah. The *shariah* is based on this very principle. If the *shariah* says something about day-to-day matters, it is to teach good behaviour. The *Shariah* prohibits whatever leads to strife. It makes obligatory that which is essential. It disapproves of that which is frivolous and approves of that which is beneficial. Since this is the stand of the *shariah*, people are free to buy, sell, and lease as they wish, just as they are free to eat and to drink what they want as long as it is not *haram,* i.e. prohibited by Allah.

In Islam making lawful what is *haram* and making unlawful what is lawful, or *halal,* is like negating the authority of Allah and denying His Absolute power. To make lawful and to prohibit is the right of Allah.

The Quran says:

"You shall not falsely declare: "This is *halal* and that is *haram*', in order to fabricate a lie against Allah; assuredly, those who fabricate a lie against Allah shall never prosper." (Surah 16:116)

Prohibiting something which is *halal* is similar to comitting *shirk*. It is not the task of any human being to decide what is to be allowed and what is to be prohibited for mankind. Allah is merciful to His servants: He makes things *halal* and *haram* for a reason, with people's well-being in view. Accordingly, Allah has neither permitted anything except what is pure, nor has He prohibited anything except what is impure. A Muslim is not required to know exactly what is unclean or harmful in what Allah has prohibited; it may be hidden from him, but be apparent to some one else, or its harm may not be discovered during his lifetime, but may be understood at a later period. What is required of a Muslim is simply to say, "We have heard and we shall obey." Allah has made *halal* all things which are good and wholesome. Allah says in the Quran: "They ask you what is lawful to them (as food). Say: Whatever is good is lawful to you…." (Surah 5:4)

Another Islamic principle is that if something is prohibited, anything which leads to is likewise prohibited. Islam intends to block all avenues leading to what is *haram*. For example, as Islam prohibits sex outside marriage, it has also prohibited anything which leads to or makes it attractive, such as seductive clothing, private meetings and casual mixing between men and women, the depiction of nudity, pornographic literature, obscene songs and so on.

Islam also declares *haram* actions which falsely represents the *haram* as *halal*. Islam has made explicit what is *halal* and what is *haram*. Therefore, one must do what is lawful and avoid what is prohibited. As regards such actions as are doubtful, Islam considers it best to avoid doing such things. It considers it an act of piety to avoid doing what is doubtful in order to stay clear of doing something *haram*. In such situations a Muslim has to be cautious, far-sighted and knowledgeable to understand such matters clearly. This is underscored by a famous saying of the Prophet ﷺ, "To acquire knowledge of *deen* is a duty of all Muslims (both men and women)." This knowledge increases one's understanding and one can thus be better equipped to take decisions in such doubtful situations.

In Islam things are prohibited only because they are impure or harmful. If something is entirely harmful, it is *haram*, and if it is entirely beneficial it is *halal*. If the harm it does outweighs its benefits, it is *haram*, while if its benefits outweigh its harm, it is *halal*. Islam has prohibited only such things as are unnecessary and dispensable, while providing alternatives which are better and which give greater ease and comfort to human beings. Whatever is *halal* is sufficient, while whatever is *haram* is superfluous.

Allah has prohibited usury, but has encouraged profitable trade. He has prohibited gambling, but has permitted betting on horse or camel-racing. Allah has prohibited men from wearing silk, but has given them the choice of other materials such as wool, linen and cotton. Allah has prohibited adultery, fornication and homosexuality, but has encouraged lawful marriage. He has prohibited intoxicating drinks in order that people may enjoy other delicious drinks which are wholesome for the body and mind. Likewise, He has prohibited unclean food but provides alternative wholesome food. Thus we see that if Allah limits the choice of His servants in relation to some things, He provides them with a still wider range of more wholesome alternatives in relation to other things of a similar kind.

EXERCISES

1. Fill in the blanks

a. Those whom Allah loves, give food on a day of privation to the orphan with claims of _____. (relationship / happiness)

b. The Quran relates those who deny the Day of Judgment with those who _____. (rejects orphans / are not good in society)

c. If the shariah says something about day-to-day matters, it is to teach _____. (good behavior / Islam)

d. Islam also declares haram actions which falsely represents the _____. (haram as halal / halal as haram)

e. To acquire knowledge of deen is a duty of _____. (every men / all muslims)

f. Allah has prohibited gambling, _____. (but has permitted betting on horse / and also prohibited betting on horse)

2. True or False

a. Islam is indifferent to the rights of the child.

b. Making lawful what is unlawful, or *haram,* and making unlawful what is lawful, or *halal,* is acceptable in Islam.

c. The Islamic *shariah* tells us how to deal with day-to-day matters in our lives.

d. Islam does not prohibit all things that are impure or harmful.

e. Allah has prohibited usury.

f. The wearing of silk for men is appropriate in Islam.

3. Answer the following questions

a. Write a brief note on the rights of the orphan in Islam.

b. What is the basis of *haram* and *halal* in Islam?

c. Why is prohibiting something which is *halal* similar to comitting *shirk*?

d. Write down the verses of the Quran relating to the orphan, *haram* and *halal.*

4. Divide the class in four groups and ask them to discuss:

a. 'Have you observed him who denies the Day of Judgment. That is one who repels the orphans.' Discuss the above Surah and how the rights of orphans highlight Islamic principles of establishing equality and justice in the society.

b. Discuss the application of the concept of Haram and Halal in the day to day life and how their observances help in the establishment of a harmonious society. After the discussion each group should read out its report in the class and every student should write in their notebooks what they have understood from the discussions.

Chapter 11   # Man's Accountability

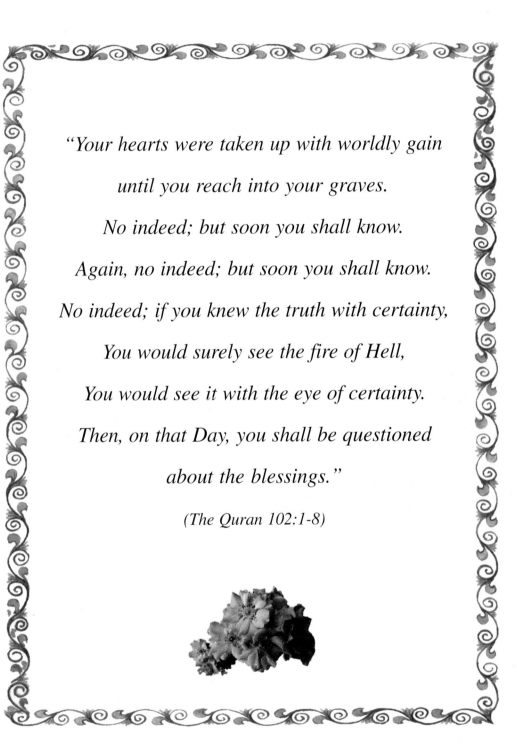

"Your hearts were taken up with worldly gain

until you reach into your graves.

No indeed; but soon you shall know.

Again, no indeed; but soon you shall know.

No indeed; if you knew the truth with certainty,

You would surely see the fire of Hell,

You would see it with the eye of certainty.

Then, on that Day, you shall be questioned

about the blessings."

(The Quran 102:1-8)

This surah of the Quran is a powerful admonition
of man's unbounded greed for worldly gain,
which preoccupies his heart and soul
until he reaches the grave.
Man wants to earn more and more
so that he may accumulate more and more goods
and material comforts.
He is totally immersed in that thought
only until he is dead.
At that time he comes to know that
the thing worth accumulating was something else,
while what he was bent on accumulating
was something else...
Increase in the worldly goods increases
man's accountability,
while due to his foolishness
he thinks that he is adding to
his comfort and success....

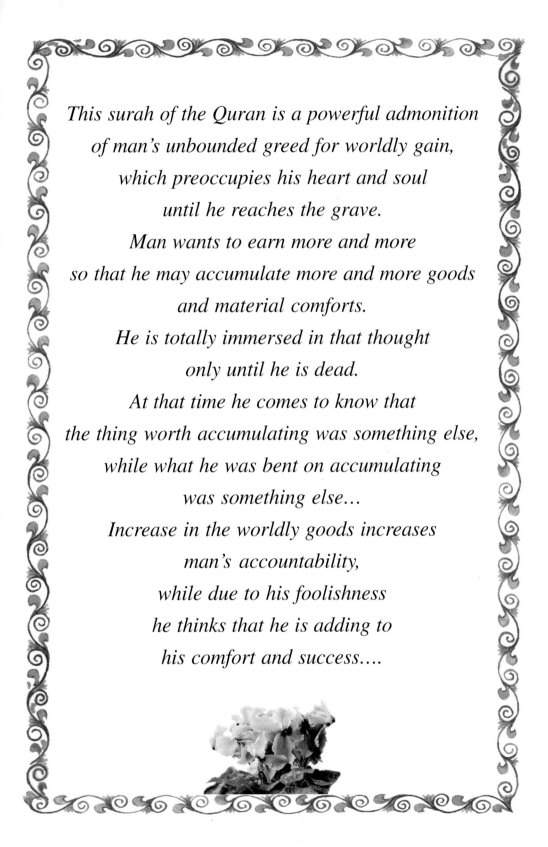

www.goodwordbooks.com

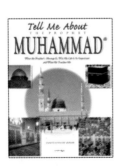

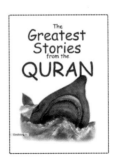